The Supernatural Entrepreneur

5 BIBLICAL PRINCIPLES TO BUILD YOUR BUSINESS WITH GOD

CHANEL E MARTIN

BEYOND
THE
BOOK MEDIA

References for Scripture Quotations

Unless noted otherwise, all scriptures are taken from the Holy Bible, New Living Translation, copyright C 1996, 2004, 2007 by Tyndale House Foundation. Used by permission of Tyndale House Publishers, Inc. Carol Stream, IL 60188. All rights reserved.

Scripture taken from *The Message*. Copyright 1993, 1994, 1995, 1996, 2000, 2001, 2002. Used by permission of NavPress Publishing Group.

Scripture quotations marked (NLT) are taken from the Holy Bible, New Living Translation, copyright C 1996, 2004, 2007 by Tyndale House Foundation. Used by permission of Tyndale House Publishers, Inc. Carol Stream, IL 60188. All rights reserved.

———

ISBN –978-1-953788-73-3 **(Printed)**

ISBN –978-1-953788-75-7 **(E-Book)**

Contents

Acknowledgments

I would like to acknowledge my amazing team at Beyond The Book Media for publishing my book. I would also like to acknowledge all of my KBN Kousins at Kingdom Business Network for trusting my voice and believing in me. And finally, I would like to thank everyone in Chanel's Book Review group that took the time to read my book and give me amazing feedback.

Introduction

My name is Chanel E. Martin. And if you are wondering, the E. is important. At one time, I went by Chanel E'bone on everything. When God began shifting me into ministry, He told me to change my name. I was no longer Chanel E'bone but now Chanel E. Martin. I should have known my life would go through some major transitions after my name change. The Supernatural Entrepreneur shares the principles I learned over the years as a bonafide, Holy Spirit, faith-filled, prophetic business owner. I couldn't do business any old way. I had to partner with God and have supernatural faith!

Chanel E. Martin is a woman of many different facets. I am a wife, a mother of 4 (we are done btw before you ask), an ordained minister, and a serial entrepreneur. I started my entrepreneurial journey in

2009 and was called to marketplace ministry in December 2015. I believe God uniquely purposed me to help Kingdom Entrepreneurs build their businesses in God's way. In order to build your business with God, you will have to operate in the supernatural.

So, what exactly qualifies me for this journey? Like many of you, I started my entrepreneurship journey lost. I knew I had a word from God (or a burning desire, you might call it) to be my own boss. Yes, that's what I called being an entrepreneur. I could be my own boss, go ahead and laugh out loud! But I soon realized that it was so much more than that. I didn't have the language to describe what I was experiencing, but I knew that I needed God. My relationship with God was the only way that I got through entrepreneurship.

My relationship with God included lots and lots of prayer, inner healing, and understanding what the Bible had to say about entrepreneurship. As a first-generation business owner, all of this was new territory for me. My mother didn't understand, my father was just as clueless, and I was the first of my immediate friends to attempt to build a "real" business.

I launched my first "real" company in 2012, Techturized Inc., also known as Myavana, and by the "world's" standards, we were winning. We had national recognition, investors, and an all-star team of scientists and engineers who attended the prestigious Georgia Institute of Technology. We created what was probably the world's first hair product recommendation engine. And the world loved what we were doing.

But something was missing! I felt lost, confused, and frustrated. From the outside looking in, we were perfect, but if you looked under the hood, you'd see that we were struggling. When I say struggling, I am not talking about financially but spiritually and emotionally. The weight of entrepreneurship was taking its toll on me. As a believer, I knew God had more for me and my business, but I couldn't figure out what I was missing.

And so… I began to toil. I was throwing the dart and wishing for it to land. Needless to say, God had me step down in 2016 to help other entrepreneurs who felt just like me. Those who knew God had called them to start their business were stuck figuring out how to grow and scale. God began to deal with me about specific principles. Principles that, when applied to my business, would help me stay in the will of God and see the financial fruits of my labor.

This book aims to give you the biblically-based principles God shared with me along my journey. And at the time of my writing this book, God has entrusted me to share these principles with over 100,000 entrepreneurs through my 3rd company, Beyond The Book Media, and my marketplace ministry, Kingdom Business Network.

I pray that you read each principle and pray into how God desires you to apply it to your business for the stage of your business. Some of these new principles will be old concepts present in familiar ways or new strategies that you can't wait to implement. The main goal is to go from reading to action and apply them to your business.

If you love this book, you can visit www.supernaturalentrepreneur.co for additional resources, listen to our podcast, and connect with me!

I present to you The Supernatural Entrepreneur!

Don't Do It Scared, Do It In Faith

E ntrepreneurship can be a scary place. Most of you reading this are probably first-generation business owners. You are taking a risk by jumping into the murky waters of small business ownership. It takes some crazy faith to do something you've never done before and to create something you have never seen. Somehow you have to muster the courage to do it anyway despite everything in you telling you to quit. Society has repeatedly told us that no matter how we feel, we should do it scared!

Do it scared. Don't let the fact that you are afraid hold you back from achieving your dreams. We've said it over and over. We've indoctrinated it into our mindset and as a part of our culture. Do it scared. It's the phrase that will help you launch into the deep, right? But what if I told you that as a Kingdom Entrepreneur, doing it scared is actually out of the will of God. What if I told you that God never ever instructs us to do anything afraid. What if I told you that you are probably limiting your success by inviting and saving space for fear in your process! Doing it scared is a myth and a worldly construct that Christians should not adhere to. We must be careful with the idioms and mantras we adopt as part of our routines.

Think about it. How often have you gone to do something, afraid and nervous, and you said to yourself that you were going to do it scared? How often have you encouraged a friend or family member to do something scared? Probably more times than you can remember. Doing it scared does NOT mean that you WILL NOT be successful in what you have set out to achieve. Doing it scared does NOT mean that you will fail either. What doing it scared and accepting fear as a part of your process does, is invite the enemy to build alongside you. We should never do anything with fear because fear is from hell. Period! Doing it with fear literally means doing it with Satan. If you think I am reaching, keep reading.

For God has not given us a spirit of fear and timidity, but of power, love, and self-discipline. [2 Timothy 1:7 NLT]

2 Timothy 1:7 clearly states that God has not given us a spirit of fear. Now, if our heavenly father is the creator of all things good, perfect, and lovely. The one who created heaven and earth and all that inhabits it, why was it necessary for Apostle Paul to let us know that God did not give us a spirit of fear? If God did not give us a spirit of fear, then the only giver of fear has to be Satan himself! Hell gives us fear to keep us from producing and operating in our God-given purpose. Hell desires to scare you out of your promise. And if you are doing it afraid, you have forfeited the promises of God and come into agreement with hell.

I know this revelation might shock you, or maybe your spirit quickly agrees with this. If we are not to do it in fear, what are we supposed to do when God asks us to do something that we are literally afraid to do? God has a history of telling us to do things that make our natural minds and bodies tense in fear. You are not the first person God has given an assignment that appeared impossible or would bring forth great opposition.

I was a big cheerleader for the phrase "do it afraid." In fact, I created a viral meme on social media about doing it scared. I believed my success was predicated on the fact that I did it afraid. I boasted about not letting fear stop me from achieving what I set out to accomplish even though I was afraid. I believed that fear was inevitable and that you would have it no matter what.

I remember one day, a young lady attempted to correct me by sending me a direct message via one of my social media accounts. She stated that I didn't have to fear and was wrong to say I would always have it. Annoyed by her correction, I immediately told her I disagreed with her and went on about my day. It wasn't until a few months later, after reading the book of Joshua, that the light bulb went off.

Holy Spirit whispered to me, "I never told you to do it in fear." Stunned by this revelation, I began recounting the numerous Bible stories I had heard. Absolutely nowhere does the word of God gives instructions to do anything afraid. I realized that I had been spreading a lie to God's people unbeknownst to me, and I quickly repented. Because God uses me to help push people into destiny, the enemy used my ignorance to tell people to invite fear into their God-given purpose, which was wrong and not Biblical.

Many thoughts ran through my mind, was I not successful because I did it afraid? How many people are living by this phrase and reciting it daily? What would have changed about my process if I had not done it afraid? What was I supposed to do to overcome the fear and anxiety I would experience when venturing into the unknown or new territory? If you have those questions, keep reading. Your answers are soon to come.

One of my favorite Bible characters is Joshua. When I started walking in purpose, the Lord told me I had a Joshua anointing. I began to study the book of Joshua as a roadmap for my purpose journey. In Joshua Chapter 1:1-9, we learn that Moses has died, and it is now Joshua's time to lead the people into the promised land. God has now called Joshua to carry out the mandate handed to him by Moses.

Then Moses summoned Joshua and said to him in the presence of all Israel, "Be strong and courageous, for you must go with this people into the land that the Lord swore to their ancestors to give them, and you must divide it among them as their inheritance. 8 The Lord himself goes before you and will be with you; he will never leave you nor forsake you. Do not be afraid; do not be discouraged."
[Deuteronomy 31:7-8, NIV]

Moses shares four notable things we need to apply when operating in purpose, especially in our businesses.

- He first tells Joshua to be strong and courageous
- God will go before him and will be with him
- God will never leave or forsake Joshua
- Don't be afraid or discouraged

Joshua had the monumental task of leading thousands of Israelites into the promised land without his mentor Moses. He had to do it without him, and I am sure fear arose when Joshua was handed the assignment. Moses never says, I know you are afraid, but do it scared anyway. No, Moses tells Joshua that you will need to be strong and courageous before you do anything! And God has mandated that you do the same.

In Psalms 23:4, we are instructed that even though we are to walk through uncertain times, we are to have no fear. We are to pursue all things with the confidence that God is with us, and therefore, we shall fear not! No matter the state or circumstance of your business, you can come out of agreement with fear and trust that, just like Joshua, God has already gone before you and will not leave or forsake you.

Yea, though I walk through the valley of the shadow of death,

I will fear no evil;
For You are with me;
Your rod and Your staff, they comfort me. [Psalm 23:4,
NKJV]

In 1 Chronicles 28:20, David is speaking with his son Solomon. Solomon was awarded the task of building the temple for God. David was giving Solomon a divine assignment, which was a massive undertaking. After David gave Solomon the instructions for building the temple, he immediately told Solomon to be strong and courageous and not be discouraged. How could Solomon tap into supernatural strength and courage? It was because God would be with him, and he didn't have to worry about failing or God leaving him.

Then David continued, "Be strong and courageous, and do the work. Don't be afraid or discouraged, for the Lord God, my God, is with you. He will not fail you or forsake you. He will see to it that all the work related to the Temple of the Lord is finished correctly. [1 Chronicles 28:20]

Have you thought about projects that you have started but ended up "failing"? Did you do them afraid? Did you do them without God? How often have we created and built something that didn't work out as we intended and got angry with God? How often did you not get the desired results and grow frustrated with God? Did you do it with courage and strength, or were you afraid and unsure? Something supernatural must happen when you decide to come out of agreement with fear and do it with faith. And by doing it with faith, you step into courage, boldness, and the strength needed for success.

How To Do It Unscared

You will need to activate your faith. And if you can't seem to muster up the faith, you can tap into the faith of someone that has gone before you and achieved success.

I remember your genuine faith, for you share the faith that first filled your grandmother Lois and your mother, Eunice. And I know that same faith continues strong in you. 6 This is why I remind you to fan into flames the spiritual gift God gave you when I laid my hands on you. 7 For God has not given us a spirit of fear and timidity, but of power, love, and self-discipline. [2 Timothy1:5-7, NLT]

Paul reminded Timothy to come out of agreement with fear and tap into the faith that his grandmother and mother, Eunice, operated in. Timothy was charged with continuing Apostle Paul's assignment without fear and timidity. Basically, Paul told Timothy, "You are not new to this. You are true to this!" I am telling you that no matter the assignment, you have accomplished something in your life that you can pull in the remembrance of the faith it took to achieve success.

Once you have pulled on the faith to get started, you need to be strong and courageous. Depending on the assignment or opportunity, you, in your natural self, do not possess the strength or courage needed for the assignment. That is why fear is the next response after we assess what we've been asked to achieve. But what if I told you that God knows you are not strong, wise, or intelligent enough. If you were, you wouldn't need Him to be with you along the journey. We learn how to pull supernatural in 2 Corinthians 12:8-10.

8 Concerning this thing, I pleaded with the Lord three times that it might depart from me. 9 And He said to me, "My grace is sufficient for you, for My strength is made perfect in weakness." Therefore most gladly, I will rather boast in my infirmities, that the power of Christ may rest upon me. 10 Therefore I take pleasure in infirmities, in reproaches, in needs, in persecutions, in distresses, for

Christ's sake. For when I am weak, then I am strong. [2 Corinthians 12:8-10, NKJV]

Before you can draw strength, you must first acknowledge that you need it. Instead of saying I am afraid, how about saying, Father, I need to be strengthened. Once you admit you are weak, you can take on God's grace. The grace to be strengthened only happens when we admit we are weak. As easy as this concept is, it is one powerful approach that is overlooked. This forces us to pause and take a moment to call out to God in our weaknesses. In this hustle-and-grind society, we can be guilty of attempting to outwork our weaknesses. God loves empty and weak vessels that can be filled with His perfect strength.

God has a perfect strength and power cocktail needed for the job, but you have got to come to Him to get it. And guess what? It's going to be different for each assignment! The strength cocktail needed for the previous engagement could have changed due to new requirements. God will strengthen you, but you have to sit still and trust Him to receive it.

Now it's time for you to be fearless and not led by discouragement! Both Joshua and Solomon were instructed by their predecessors to not be afraid! I believe it takes faith and strength to combat the fear that hell would try to attach to your business and kingdom assignment. It's probably nearly impossible to attack fear without faith and supernatural strength. Your scary self is not your best self. Your fearless self is unstoppable. I want you to recall a time in your life or business in which you were not afraid. A time when you were confident in your ability to succeed. When you are confident, you show up to the job differently. You approach the task with a winner's mindset. You believe in your ability to tackle what God has purposed you to do.

Your scarry self will typically show up timid and unwilling to give it all you've got for fear of failure, discouragement, or disappointment. You may actually step out and do it, but it is not with the full grace and strength God has ordained for you. I believe we don't see the desired results initially because of how we showed up. When you are afraid, you are unable to put your best foot forward. You are unable to show up in Godly excellence.

Doing it scared, aside from inviting hell into your process, also means that you are possibly doing it:

- Without faith
- With fear
- Unconfident in your ability to reach success

- Timid
- Without the grace and strength assigned to the job

Imagine being given a job as a baker and you show up to an empty room with no oven and ingredients to bake with. That is what happens when you do it scared. You have forfeited the necessary tools to complete the job!

The next time you are faced with an assignment, new business venture, or Kingdom mandate that would typically cause you to be afraid, please do the following. First, you will need to activate your faith. Remember that last thing you accomplished, or if you know someone that has achieved a similar level of success, receive their faith for yourself. Let your faith ignite your path forward. Once your faith has been activated, admit all the areas in your assignment where you are weak. What areas are you afraid of failing in? There you will find your weakness.

You can pray this:

Father, I am weak in (list all the areas). I need your supernatural strength to complete (list the assignment). Your Word says that your grace is sufficient and that your strength is perfect in my weakness. Father, I need your perfect strength to be applied to every weakness.

I come out of agreement with fear. God, I am in need of fearless strength and power for the assignment. Lord, I am making a decision to operate in boldness and leave timidity behind. I come against discouragement and disappointment and receive that you, God, are with me. Lord, I am settling in my heart that no matter what the outcome is, God, you will not fail me and that if you assigned it to me, then you, God, are with me. In Jesus' name, I pray. Amen

If you can practice the above prayer strategy and apply it to your life and business, I can almost assure you that you will see success. I believe that favor and abundance will chase you down. God does not give you assignments for you to fail. Failing is a decision that is made outside of the will of God. Today, right now, remind yourself that you will not fail. You will no longer operate or do anything God has given you with fear but with fearless faith!

Your Faith Matters, Your Feelings Don't

Your Faith Matters

One of the most used by highly misinterpreted scriptures in entrepreneurship is "faith without works is dead" James 2:17. Although we all know and understand this concept, it's one that many believers struggle to actually follow through on. I don't know if it's because we like the idea of a thing and not the process or if many of us are still treating our faith like it's magic. And honestly, I am not even mad or surprised. Rhetoric like "faith it till you make it," or "wait on God," or "just believe" will have you reciting James 2:17 in one breath but operating in the exact opposite.

One day, frustrated with what several of my friends and family were experiencing, I went to God for answers. I asked Him this one question: "Why weren't my friends and family members experiencing breakthroughs? It seemed as if nothing they did would produce the fruit they desired. I saw repeated cycles of "failed" attempts, and as a natural strategist and problem solver, I felt helpless.

God replied with an answer in a way I had never encountered. God explained that most people did not understand that it wasn't just faith without works was dead, but it was faith = works. As a math enthusiast and chemical engineer by trade, I love equations. So, I pulled out my notebook and asked God to tell me more! God broke down the concept that any old work attached to faith would not yield a breakthrough.

You can have BIG faith but little works. In fact, that is the story with most people struggling to see results. Their faith is on 5000, but when you check their works, they have completed the bare minimum. But because there was some effort put towards the goal, they classify that as work! So, they do some "work" and get angry when the "work" they put in doesn't yield the results that they had "faith for."

I am not excluding the possibility of God performing miracles in your business and life, but your business strategy should not include a miracle bail-out plan from God. You need your faith in business. You won't get very far if you don't have it, but you also need a work ethic to match what you are believing in God for. It's more than just having the faith for it.

You will only work as much as your faith allows! Your faith will dictate how much you work! If you were led to believe that if you showed up to work every day at a specific time, you would become a multimillionaire after 30 days, what would you do? I know exactly what you would do. You would make sure you made it to work on time without missing a day. Multimillions are on the line, and you are not going to pass up that opportunity. You wouldn't just show up to work one day and then say, "I'm believing in God and that I am going to be a multimillionaire," and decide to never go back to work again. You will do exactly what it takes to yield the desired results.

In business, most of us are aware that if we stay consistent, make improvements when necessary, and have faith in what we are selling, eventually, we will be successful. This concept is proven over and over by people, great and small. The amount of success is determined by the measure of faith AND work [faith = works] that was produced. We love a good overnight success story! Why? Because it feeds our ego that we don't actually have to work as much for the goals that we desire.

The book of James expresses this concept for us to understand how this faith and work thing really works.

17 Thus also faith by itself, if it does not have works, is dead. 18 But someone will say, "You have faith, and I have works." Show me your faith without your works, and I will show you my faith by my works. 19 You believe that there is one God. You do well. Even the demons believe — and tremble! 20 But do you want to know, O foolish man, that faith without works is dead? [James 2:17-20, NKJV]

Verse 17, we know and understand very well. But it is verse 18 that gives proof that the concept of faith = works is a Biblical Principle. *"Show me your faith without your works, and I will show you my faith by my works"* basically saying that you will showcase your faith in a thing by the work that you put in. They work together but need to be equal to work together as intended. It's not enough to just believe God for it. You will have to believe God for it AND work that belief until you see it happen.

Not only does your work need to match your

faith, but you need to do the right work! You may not struggle with working, but you have to ensure that your work will yield the right results and help you accomplish your goals. There is a possibility that you could have your faith on 5000 and work like a Hebrew slave in 110-degree weather and still not yield the breakthrough God intended for you.

For example, let's say you were believing God for six-figure months in your business. You have been praying and fasting, and finally, believe that six-figure months can happen for you too. You created a vision board, hired a coach, and took every course you could get your hands on, yet your results were slow or nonexistent. On the outside, looking in, you are always busy and putting in work. But when we took a closer look into the inner workings of your brand, we found that you spend 75% of your time creating standard operating procedures (SOPs).

One might agree that creating SOPs is a tool that can simplify the process of having six-figure months. But, in order to have a 6 figure anything, you are going to have to sell. You can't just create SOPs and wish that the six-figure months will come just because you created an SOP for it. So yes, you are working, but are you doing the right work. Doing the right work is necessary for the faith = works equation to work.

I believe that this is where many Christian entrepreneurs get frustrated with God. They are struggling to figure out what the right work is! There are a few ways to get wisdom on the right work. Of course, the first thing you should do is consult God and Holy Spirit for the answer. Sit down with a pen and paper and ask God to reveal what work you should do to achieve your six-figure months. Then write down what you hear, see, and feel like He is saying. I call this prophetic journaling. God may release a strategy you understand how to implement, or He may tell you to do something beyond your current abilities. If that happens, you need to seek out the information. You can do this by doing a quick Google search and seeing what you can find on the internet. You can also seek a coach or a consultant to help you bridge the knowledge gap.

Note: If you would like to learn more about prophetic journaling you can visit the supernaturalentrepreneur.co and select the prophetic journaling tab for more info. I promise, it will change your life!

In this process, God might reveal that where your

business is currently operating is not ready for six-figure months. God might redirect your goals to start working on building the infrastructure of your brand or tell you to hire a salesperson on your team. The point is this, you have the faith, but you must be committed to doing the right work. And Holy Spirit has the ability to lead you to the right work. When you allow God to direct your work, then you eliminate toiling.

Toiling is a curse and not of God. He did not give you your business for you to toil. If we are not careful, we can have faith for a thing but attach it to toiling and not working. Dictionary.com describes toiling as hard and continuous work, exhausting labor or effort. Toiling and working are not the same. Toiling will yield results, but you will be exhausted and frustrated. We are to work within our God's strength and not our human strength. When you toil, you will never reach the fullness of the blessings attached to the faith equals work.

When the right work matches that faith to produce, you will see the hand of God move. You will have supernatural backing, and your fruit will be evident. If you have found yourself working too hard, perhaps you are using your work ethic to make up where your faith lacks! How can this even be possible, you ask? Well, let's say you sat down with

God and believe that you will sell 100 books in 30 days after launching. God gives you the strategy, and your implementation is all that is needed. On day one of the launch, you are bursting with excitement, and there is no doubt that God will deliver on what He promised. You amazingly sold 20 books in a day, and it appears as if God is fulfilling His Word.

Following the plan given to you, by day 20, worry starts setting in. At this point, only 50 books are sold, and the thought settles in your mind that you need a miracle to sell the other 50. Instead of having faith in what God said, you decide to work your own plan. You add your plans on top of what God gave you. The plan includes texting all your friends, engaging on social media 5 times a day, and sending out 10 additional emails. Because of your actions, you have stepped out of God's plan and lack the faith to believe that the 50 extra books will be sold in 10 days.

Your faith is small, but your work leads you to exhaustion. Your faith does not equal your works. Your works are greater than your faith. Because you stepped out of God's plan for your book launch, your doubt becomes a self-fulfilling prophecy, and you do not sell your 100 books in 30 days as God promised. There were conditions to that promise. That promise required you to have an equal balance of faith and works. You needed to have faith that the plan (work)

God gave you would be enough to meet your goals. Thus, leading to your lack of a breakthrough in this area. You can't have one without the other. You need both! Your faith matters but your feelings don't.

Note: If you are an author and are interested in learning a strategy to sell your first 100+ books in 30 days, check out the training tab on supernaturalentrepreneur.co for an easy lesson.

Let's talk about your feelings. Your feelings can be detrimental to your faith and your work ethic. For the faith = works concept to work, your feelings must be left out of the equation. Because let me tell you a secret, you probably won't always feel like having faith or working! How often have you stopped working towards a goal, lost consistency, or quit because you didn't feel like it!

Your feelings are a guide, not a compass. Your feelings will alert you on how something affects you mentally, spiritually, or physically, but not how or when you should proceed. Your feelings are fickle and sometimes will outright lie to you about a situation. Your feelings can be influenced by temporary circumstances that will have you make permanent decisions that don't need to be made.

You cannot allow how you feel to determine how you move in business. When you are doing something you have never done before or are out of your comfort zone, your feelings will naturally fight you against your assignment. Your feelings are supposed to help you survive, so when something goes against your normal routine, your feelings may bring false alarms.

"Feelings evolved in humans for the purpose of alerting us to everyday threats to our survival. We constantly scan our environment for dangers and opportunities, to satisfy our most basic needs. We get a constant body-mind report about the state of the world through our feelings. They give us a quick assessment about whether something is good for us or bad for us and they motivate us to take action accordingly." - psychcentral.com

When you have to use your faith to produce something, you are going outside of your natural survival mechanism into the unknown. Your feelings are trying to make sense of the new environment your faith has produced and can give you an unreal assessment of danger or fear. Your feelings can cause an imbalance in the faith = works concept.

Although your feelings feel real and powerful, they are not always the best judgment callers. Your feelings may activate inaccurate emotions caused by past experiences and traumas.

Many things may produce an emotional response. Some are in the moment, others are from our past, and many people get destabilized worrying about the uncertain future. Still other emotions may be a response to mere fantasies, lies we tell ourselves that make us needlessly unhappy. They may also be a result of misunderstandings. There is no end to the amount of feeling (both positive and negative) that flows through our lives on a daily basis; the trick is to learn how to differentiate between feelings that are born out of our imagination and those that are real and verifiable. - www.psychologytoday.com

Pursuing against your feelings and emotions can be difficult, requiring discipline and practice. You can move past your feelings to produce at the faith = work level by doing the following.

MAKE UP YOUR MIND

You cannot be indecisive when applying the faith = work concept. Your mind has to be set and focused on the end goal. A decision must be made that you will see the assignment through to the end, whether it's raining or the sun is shining. You make a vow to keep going if you are having a good day or a bad day. Others' thoughts concerning your faith or the work to produce cannot dictate how you move. A made-up mind is a mind postured for success.

UNDERSTAND THE OPPOSITION WILL COME

Some people believe that when it's good, it's God. When it's not good, it's the devil. Some people believe that when opposition comes that God can't possibly be in it. This line of thinking is a lie that our feelings will tell us. Just about every notable man/woman in the bible had a promise God gave them, but they had to face opposition to get to the promise. When faced with a trial or warfare, understand that Hell does not want you to be successful. Hell's job is to make you quit before you finish. Hell desires to shift your faith so you won't do the work. Even though there will be opposition, you will be victorious if you keep the faith. When it's God, there's grace!

8 Stay alert! Watch out for your great enemy, the devil. He prowls around like a roaring lion, looking for someone to devour. [1 Peter 5:8 NLT]

13 Therefore, put on every piece of God's armor so you will be able to resist the enemy in the time of evil. Then after

the battle you will still be standing firm. [Ephesians
6:13 NLT]

KEEP THE MOMENTUM

Consistency is the key to success. You cannot be successful in something that is not bathed in consistency. When you start having faith and working your faith, you will be urged to quit. When you stay consistent, you can ride the momentum of the consistency. Your feelings will tell you, "you're tired, take a break," or "you've been doing this too long, and no results are produced," or "what you are doing doesn't matter; no one cares." If the enemy can disrupt your consistency, then he can infiltrate your faith = work strategy. It's always harder to start back up doing a thing than to suffer through and keep going.

God wants to give you the desires of your heart. In fact, God is probably the one who put them there to begin with. It is His will for success to be acquired when his plans are followed. With God's grace, the wisdom from Holy Spirit, and faith = works, we will find success!

Note: Figuring out the right work can be diffi-cult. I have a quick training that will help you quickly assess if you work = faith is unbal-anced. Head over to supernaturalentrepre-neur.co for more information

The Truth About God's Provision & Why Prosperity Is Not Guaranteed

2016 through 2019 were some of the most difficult times of my life. It was a time of pruning and learning to follow God's voice in every single way. In 2016 I decided to step down from my award-winning and nationally known tech startup for ministry. I had my "Saul to Paul" moment [Acts 9:1-19], meaning God literally called me! I was led to go on a fast because I knew God needed to tell me something. We had just had the largest TV appearance to date, and yet I felt a shift happening with me.

I obeyed the leading of Holy Spirit, and I heard Him say this: "I need you to step down from your startup to help my entrepreneurs!" Without knowing or understanding the details of the job, I said yes.

This was probably one of the most costly but also the most rewarded yes of my entire life.

As a result, God started processing me. He started sharing wisdom that "came out of nowhere." I began having encounters that would shape and mold me into the woman I am today. He also gave me such Godly wisdom that could have come only from heaven. The wisdom that was given to me would change the trajectory of my entire life and bloodline. The first principle that God shared with me and my husband was the concept of Provision Vs. Prosperity.

I am a pew baby. I grew up in church my entire life. I am no stranger to God's Word and Christianity's concepts. As an adolescent, I often heard the phrase "God will provide." Whatever you could ever need or want, God was Jehovah Jirah, my provider. It was such a staple phrase that it was engraved in my mind. God would provide for all of my needs. While this is true for your day-to-day living, it is not a concept that should be relied upon when building wealth. God does not provide wealth!! God does not provide wealth! God does not provide wealth! God is the source of our wealth, but His provision does not cover our prosperity.

Ok, I know I just ruffled up your feathers. And if you are an Apostle, Pastor, or Bible scholar, I am sure I stepped on your toes. But please, before you stop reading this book, hear me out. I am about to explain, and it will change and transform your life. Since you are still reading, let's discuss provision vs. prosperity!

According to Dictionary.com

Provision: the providing or supplying of something, especially of food or other necessities.

Prosperity: a successful, flourishing, or thriving condition, especially in financial respects; good fortune.

If you read the above definitions, you will notice there is a difference. Provision refers to necessities only! Prosperity refers to success beyond the necessities.

My husband, Christopher Martin, caused me to examine the differences. We were in a financial bind, and he came to me with a word of wisdom. He said to me as calmly and as plainly as possible and said, "Provision is different from prosperity. We've been praying and asking God for provision hoping that it would lead to prosperity, and unfortunately, it doesn't work that way. We've been thinking about it and doing it all wrong."

Earlier I told you that I was a pew baby. In fact, I have been in church much longer than my husband. As he explained the concept, I could feel offense and heat rising in my body. Surely my husband had lost his mind. My entire life, all I heard about was how God was a provider. So, he could provide prosperity if he wanted to!

As soon as the thoughts could form in my mind, the Holy Spirit started dealing with me. He reminded me of a few key scriptures that would back the concept my husband was explaining. I had to admit that my husband, for once, was right (wives, you know how hard that was)! What Chris shared was a principle that helped me to understand how Biblical wealth worked. Let's break down this concept and how you can apply it to your world!

PROVISION

A popular passage in the bible which clearly tells the story of God's provision is beautifully displayed in Exodus 16, Manna and Quail. I am about to give you the "Chanel Notes" version of this and possibly anywhere you see scripture listed. But do me this one favor, open up your Bible and read it for yourself. Also, ask God for your personalized interpretation of where you are in your life and in your business. Ok, now back to my interpretation.

So, Moses successfully delivered the Israelites out of the hand of Pharaoh. They had been traveling in the wilderness for two weeks (the NIV version says

15 days, to be exact). Although free from bondage, the Israelites felt like complaining to Moses about the lack of steak and potatoes in the wilderness! Ok, maybe not steak and potatoes, lol, but you get the point. They were frustrated that they couldn't have the "Pots of Meat" [Exodus 16: 3, NLT] they had in slavery.

So, Moses is probably rolling his eyes, thinking, "These foolish people would rather have pots of meat than freedom and their inheritance." God, you have got to help me with your kids! So, the Lord, who absolutely loves Moses, "provides" a solution to their grumbling.

4 Then the Lord said to Moses, "Look, I'm going to rain down food from heaven for you. Each day the people can go out and pick up as much food as they need for that day. I will test them in this to see whether or not they will follow my instructions. 5 On the sixth day they will gather food, and when they prepare it, there will be twice as much as usual." [Exodus 16: 5, NLT]

God agrees to provide food from heaven. Sure, it wasn't steak and potatoes, but it would provide the necessity of food for them along the journey! It was a miracle!!! Food straight from heaven in their time of need! It was right on time and just enough to get them through each day and through the weekend.

How many of you have been in a similar situation where you really needed something? Maybe you needed a certain amount of money to pay your rent, or you'd potentially get evicted. Or you needed resources for a project, and you had no idea where they would come from? You needed God to provide something that was necessary! And at what feels like the last minute, you get exactly what you need! Jehovah Jireh, God the provider, shows up. God is always going to provide for us. It's our birthright. Whatever you need, if you ask for it, He will give it to you.

13 You can ask for anything in my name, and I will do it, so that the Son can bring glory to the Father. [John 14:13 NLT]

31 "So don't worry about these things, saying, 'What will we eat? What will we drink? What will we wear?' [Matthew 6:31 NLT]

8 And God will generously provide all you need. Then you will always have everything you need and plenty left over to share with others. [2 Corinthians 9:8 NLT]

19 And this same God who takes care of me will supply all your needs from his glorious riches, which have been given to us in Christ Jesus. [Philippians 4:19 NLT]

Provision is available to all believers. As you can read in the above scriptures, our needs are already promised! All you have to do is ask. This concept should relieve you from any stressful situation you need God to provide for. He's going to do it, and He will always do it.

But here is where it gets a little interesting. If you read the scriptures and examine what is really being said, you will notice that although provision is guaranteed, prosperity is not! Many of us have spent years and years begging for provision and have grown frustrated and upset with God when prosperity doesn't show up.

Let's do a quick study on provision by examining Exodus 16 again. We know at this point that God has promised to give the Israelites manna and quail, but there were restrictions and instructions connected to the promise.

PROVISION IS TIME SENSITIVE

God promised to provide food for the Israelites under one condition. They were to only take what they needed and could not keep or store any extras. Let's apply this to your business, purpose, or life. Think about how God would always send the one client that would help you keep your business afloat at the last minute. They would show up with the right amount of money to keep you afloat. This is an example of God's provision for your business. It was time-sensitive; cue the old song "He's an On Time God" by Dottie Peoples. This song is the anthem for believers and an ode to God always providing for His children!

PROVISION IS USUALLY JUST ENOUGH

God sent manna and quail daily. The Israelites had just enough food to get them through the day. Once the day was up, they had to stretch their faith to trust God again to provide again. God will send provision on your way to prosperity! They were on a journey to the land flowing with milk and honey (prosperity) but before reaching the final destination, trusting God to provide was necessary. I believe God only gives just enough so that we won't grow comfortable and complacent with provision when He desires for your business to live in the land of milk and honey.

17 So the people of Israel did as they were told. Some gathered a lot, some only a little. 18 But when they measured it out, everyone had just enough. Those who gathered a lot had nothing left over, and those who

gathered only a little had enough. Each family had just
what it needed. [Exodus 16:17-18 NLT]

In 2019, my company, Beyond The Book Media, was only a few months old. I was in the process of planning our first summit, and when I ran the numbers, it appeared that we did not have enough money to produce the event. And guess what? The event was in a few days. In my tears and frustration, I cried out to God to help me. I realized I was only $1,000 short. I didn't know how I would get the money, but I understood that only God could help me.

Within three hours, I received a request to jump on a call with a client about her publishing package. As we approached the conclusion of the call, she asked if she could purchase one of our $1,000 packages. Yes, you read that right! God provided the exact amount of money needed to produce the event within 3 hours of me asking Him. Just like the Israelites, He provided that "manna," in my case, "money," that my business needed.

PROVISION SPOILS

Provision has an assignment and a season. I am not saying that you can only have provision for certain times in your business. I am, however, expressing that when you try to hoard provision that was intended and assigned for a specific reason, it will spoil. When God provides, we are to use it for what is needed and necessary. Provision is not to be saved or stored. It was given to you for a reason, and now we are required to use it for just that.

19 Then Moses told them, "Do not keep any of it until morning." 20 But some of them didn't listen and kept some of it until morning. But by then it was full of maggots and had a terrible smell. Moses was very angry with them. [Exodus 16:19-20 NLT]

As you can read in Exodus 16:19-20, although they were told to not keep any of it until morning, those that didn't listen woke up to a stinky and maggot-filled mess. If they would have just listened in the first place, they would have bypassed this whole experience.

How many times have you prayed and asked God to help you financially in a particular area of your business or life? When God showed up and provided, were you tempted to use the money in another area other than what it was initially intended for? I think about if I would have taken the extra $1,000 I received from my client and decided to save it and just cancel the event altogether. Or maybe took the $1,000 and used it to pay off or down some credit cards? I wonder how I could have disrupted or delayed my process by not using the money and trying to save it for another purpose.

After reading, you are probably asking yourself, "If God is not providing me prosperity, then how do I get it?" The answer to this question is found in Deuteronomy 8:18.

18 "And you shall remember the Lord your God, for it is He who gives you power to get wealth, that He may establish His covenant which He swore to your fathers, as it is this day. [Deuteronomy 8:18, NKJV]

In Deuteronomy, Moses is speaking again to the Israelites. We remember in Exodus how God provided manna and quail for the sake of context known as provision. In Deuteronomy, Moses moves beyond provision and into the prosperity that was promised. He explains that God gives "the power to get wealth, that He may establish His covenant." This scripture is loaded with revelation about prosperity. Let's take a look at it.

YOU'RE GOING TO HAVE TO WORK FOR IT

I hate to burst your bubble, and you may even disagree with me on this one, but you have to work for prosperity, aka wealth. Now provision is automatic and distributed to every believer, but prosperity is not. Moses didn't say that God is going to give you wealth. He said that God gives you the power to get wealth.

Dictionary.com describes power as ability to do or act; capability of doing or accomplishing something. So, in essence, God gives you the ability to do or accomplish wealth. He has and will place everything inside you so that you can be a wealth-producing machine! He supplies the power, and you produce the work.

The biblical description of power relates primarily to God and people. Power is an inherent characteristic of God. It is the result of his nature. God's kind of power is seen in his creation. His inexplicable power is the only explanation for the virgin birth of Jesus. Power is always a derived characteristic for people, who receive power from God. - Biblestudytools.com

Please do not confuse the power with toiling. Nowhere does the scripture mean that you are going to have to toil or struggle, but you are, sweetheart, going to have to work! This is why winning the lottery or acquiring some large sum of money quickly hardly ever pans out for the best. I'll admit, I have been guilty of just wishing and praying for wealth to fall upon my lap like manna and quail, and it never seemed to work out in my favor! This line of thinking is faulty and not Biblical. I am sure you can name one person where money and wealth just found them. But if you took a closer look into their life, if they didn't have to work to get it, they are going to have to work to keep it.

PROSPERITY IS PROMISED

You've accepted that you have to work for your prosperity, but I need you to understand that your prosperity is a promise from God. It was a covenant that was given to our ancestors. You, me, Oprah, Bill Gates, all of us as believers of Jesus Christ, have access to prosperity. How is this possible? When we accept Jesus Christ as our Lord and Savior, we are now heirs to the inheritance that was promised to Abraham.

29 And now that you belong to Christ, you are the true

children of Abraham. You are his heirs, and God's promise
to Abraham belongs to you. [Galatians 3:29 NLT]
16 So the promise is received by faith. It is given as a free
gift. And we are all certain to receive it, whether or not we
live according to the law of Moses, if we have faith like
Abraham's. For Abraham is the father of all who believe.
[Romans 4:16 NLT]
6 I will make you extremely fruitful. Your descendants will
become many nations, and kings will be among them! 7 "I
will confirm my covenant with you and your
descendants[a] after you, from generation to generation.
This is the everlasting covenant: I will always be your God
and the God of your descendants after you. [Genesis
17:6-7 NLT]

As a believer, the concept of prosperity and
wealth being promised to me was mind-blowing. I
thought wealth was only for a few "special people,"
and maybe I just didn't make the cut. So why aren't
more people accessing their prosperity? For many are
called, but few are chosen [Matthew 22:14 NLT].
Many are called to prosperity, but only a few will use
the power given to them to produce wealth.

WHAT ARE YOU GOING TO DO WITH THIS PRINCIPLE?

When my husband, Chris, introduced the concept to me, a lightbulb went off! I began examining my mindset and behavior around prosperity. When you know better, you are now equipped to do better. I realized that I was praying, planning, and positioning my business for God's provision. Provision was all I knew and asked for, so in turn, it was all that I received. Now I fix my heart, vision, and actions toward prosperity.

Provision gives you just what you need. And many of you have been stuck in your "provision" or "just enough" season. You know that God has more for you, but you can't figure out how to move past this hump. Provision promised quail, not prime rib steak. Provision will ensure you have a roof over your head, not a multimillion-dollar estate. Provision gives you a strategy to stay afloat, not continuous overflow in your business or brand. Provision is to keep you sustained along your journey to prosperity.

Prosperity will produce timeless overflow in assigned areas of your life and business. It will last generations and was promised to all believers, but we will have to use our God-given power to access prosperity, our birthright. Let's start by coming out of agreement with the mindset that provision is all God has for our business. Let's believe that God is a God of generational overflow and abundance. From now on, we will target our prayers, thoughts, and actions toward prosperity building.

PROSPERITY BUILDING ACTIVITIES

Partnering with God in prayer to release prosperity for your business and life

Partnering with God in prayer may sound a bit abstract, but I am going to give you a strategy that works for me. First, I ask God for everything! Literally every single thing. Before you make a decision for your business, go to God in prayer and wait for an answer. I practice prophetic journaling. It's a process of asking God questions and writing down what you see, feel, hear, or what drops in your spirit, and writing it down. You can purchase a prophetic journal by visiting Godblessthescribe.com.

Writing it down removes the friction of trying to figure out if it's you or if it's God. I've taught thousands of entrepreneurs this method, which has been life changing. Ask God for prosperity and fruit-bearing activities you can do daily in your business. When you pray, pray to release, but also pray to get answers. There are many things God will give you an immediate response for!

Note: If you would like to learn more about prophetic journaling you can visit the supernatura-lentrepreneur.co and select the prophetic journaling tab for more info. I promise, it will change your life!

Understanding that God will provide, but He also has so much more to offer than "just enough."

We broke down this concept earlier, but I will remind you here. Remember that you have to make a choice to believe God for more. Ask, and ye shall receive, right? So, if you are only asking for just enough, you shall receive just enough. But what if you believe beyond what you need. What if you targeted your faith for the impossible! It will probably be challenging at first, but consistent practice will become part of your prayer vocabulary. I want you to ask God for 10X what you need! Watch Him deliver.

Begin using the power (your gifts, talents, abilities, favor, grace) that God has given you.

What has God given you that you are currently not using, or what could you maximize to build prosperity for your family? Us Christian Entrepreneurs are guilty of operating out of false humility! False humility looks like giving away every single product and service away for free or at a low cost. It looks like feeling guilty for making money from what comes easy to you. It can also manifest as fear of success. You want to stay hidden and are afraid of being in the forefront. Trust me, I have had to struggle with each area. But when you use your power, you are connecting yourself to prosperity!

Have the Mindset That You Can and Will Move from Provision Only to Prosperity

Listen, if you don't believe it for yourself, it will not happen for you. If you really believe, then it really will happen for you. It's that simple. You will have to make a decision that you will be prosperous. I don't care if you have negative fifty cents in your bank account right now. This principle still holds true.

7 For as he thinketh in his heart, so is he: Eat and drink, saith he to thee; but his heart is not with thee. [Proverbs 23:7, KJV]

I started doing daily Biblical affirmations to help

me remember to keep a prosperous mindset. Here are a few you can use to get started!

I declare that the Lord my God will make me successful in everything I put my hands to. I will be fruitful in every aspect of my life and live in abundance and overflow. The Lord will pass these blessings through my entire bloodline! [Deuteronomy 30:9]

I declare that at this very moment, what has been made available to me in the spirit will manifest in the natural. All the blessings, resources, healing, finances, and whatever else I'm in need of from my Heavenly Father's Kingdom will come to me soon. His will for my life will come to pass on earth as it is in heaven. [Matthew 6:10]

I declare that my God, who began the good work within me, my family, my finances, my business, and my relationships, will continue His work until it is finally finished. [Philippians 1:6] My God is a promise keeper and A finisher!

I declare that I will receive everything I ask of you, God, for my family, my finances, my health, and my relationships. Everything that I am looking for and am in need of, I will find. Every door to my destiny and purpose that I knock on will be opened up to me. [Matthew 7:7-8]

I declare that the work of my hands will produce great wealth and that I will leave an inheritance for my children's children. [Proverbs 13:22]

I declare that as my God has done for Isaac, He will also do for me. Everything I've sown this year and in past seasons will be returned to me 100-fold before the end of this year! [Genesis 26:12]

Poverty Products and Prosperity Products, and Why Understanding the Difference Matters

N ow that you understand the difference between provision and prosperity, let's apply it directly to your business, ministry, or brand. I would like to introduce a concept to you that will change how you create, launch and sell products for your business. Let's talk about prosperity vs. poverty products. Yes, there is a difference in the types of products you can create for your business, and the motive and intent behind it matters.

We all typically become entrepreneurs for three reasons. A) You want to solve a problem you have faced or recognized as a market gap. B) You want to change the world and help people. C) You need to make some money and survive. However, if you found your way to entrepreneurship, you will find the following principle helpful as you begin to grow and scale your business.

POVERTY PRODUCTS

Poverty products are created out of desperation, confusion, frustration, fear, and anxiety. God never instructs us to carry out our Kingdom assignments from a place of fear.

This is my command—be strong and courageous! Do not be afraid or discouraged. For the Lord your God is with you wherever you go." [Joshua 1:9 NLT]

Poverty products are typically a means to an end and an opportunity to make money quickly. Poverty products are hardly ever all the way thought out, nor are they properly planned and produced. Poverty products are typically unoriginal and are very short-lived. Poverty products hardly ever produce prosperity. I am not saying that poverty products do not have their place or season in business, especially if you need money right now. However, they should not be part of your business ecosystem long term.

So, you read the word poverty and are probably thinking, "Have I ever produced a poverty product?"

Well, let's talk through a few examples. Some of your poverty products are great products, but you have mispriced them due to a poverty mindset, or you are trying to sell quickly to meet an urgent need. I, too, have sold poverty products.

I remember when I first launched the publishing side of Beyond The Book Media! As an Indie publisher, I was new to selling premium four and five-figure services. My business coach urged me to get into selling higher-end products and told me that the price could not be less than $999.00. Afraid of rejection and unsure if anyone would buy a publishing package from me as a newbie, I sold publishing packages for $997.

I had a $1,500-a-month coaching bill I had to cover and figured that if I only sold three packages, I would cover the bill and have a little left over to pay operating expenses. I offered my "self-publishing" packages to my audience and sold 7 of them in one week! I was surprised to sell as many as I did and was grateful and afraid at the same time. I priced my packages at about $2,500 lower than the competition and figured this would be an easy way to enter the market.

Well, I was right, but I was wrong... very wrong. Now, I am extremely grateful for the 7 clients that purchased those first packages from me. That was the seed for the company we are now, but I learned a few very expensive lessons. The first lesson was that I valued my product way too low! At $997, I could hardly cover the contractor fees I had to pay to get the book edited, formatted, and the cover designed. I had an extremely low profit margin. I was making money but unable to really keep the money we were making.

The second lesson I learned was that it attracted less-than-ideal clients. The client who wanted the lower pricing was not a good fit for our brand and bank account. I started noticing a particular trend in the clients we were attracting. They did not want to adhere to our company's culture and put stress on myself and my team. It ended up being a nightmare. Frustrated, annoyed, and feeling stuck, I had to make a change.

The blessing of the Lord makes a person rich, and he adds no sorrow with it. [Proverbs 10:22]

The third lesson I learned was that I did not understand my value and expertise. I was thinking too small. I had to learn that I could not serve the customers in the best manner with lower-tiered pricing. I could not afford to hire more help because there was no room in the budget per book. I also was aiming too low for my revenue goals. I just wanted to pay my $1,500-a-month coaching fees; everything else was a bonus. So, I treated my business just like that.

I was not positioning my revenue goals, products, and services for prosperity. I presented them only to make ends meet and to keep the company afloat. Approximately 6 months later, I knew I had to make a change. I needed to transition from offering a poverty product to a prosperity product. I needed to raise my prices if I wanted my company to meet the first milestone of 6 figures. And I did just that!

I took a look at our best clients. I asked myself the following questions: Who were my best-paying clients? What clients did I enjoy working with? What types of books moved quickly through our process? After I had the answers to these questions, I changed my marketing to speak directly to that audience and raised my prices.

I can admit I was afraid that I was making a mistake. They were used to purchasing products at $997, and now I was asking for $2,997! But that year, I tripled my prices and tripled my revenue for the year! It was that simple, I moved out of the poverty mindset and began positioning Beyond The Book Media for prosperity. And we are growing exponentially year after year.

I often asked myself, what if I had started out of the gate with packages priced at $2,997? I did not have the mindset or confidence to even believe someone would spend that money with me. I took a product God gave me to set me up for prosperity and made it a poverty product. Although it was not a poverty product, my mindset made it that way.

Here is another example of poverty products. I remember my family had just moved into our home, and I was pregnant with our 3rd child. My husband's contract had ended, and he was unemployed for a few months before landing another job. We spent months living off our savings, and that money ran out with our move. I felt as though we needed a money miracle.

Like most natural-born hustlers, I started thinking about what I could sell or provide as a six-month pregnant woman. I came up with an idea: sell a course on fundraising for your business. I was successful at raising money with my very first business. Having helped raise a half-million dollars, I knew somebody wanted to learn how to do it. I hit the ground running and started putting together the course. I created a graphic and began promoting the $49 class on social media.

I shared it on every platform that I had a presence on. I was hoping to make a few thousand dollars to help offset some of our expenses during the move. But to my surprise, I sold ZERO seats. Yes, ZERO seats. Hurt and confused, I couldn't understand why God would set me up for failure like that. He knew we needed money, and I was angry. What were we going to do now? My plan had failed.

In tears, I calmed down enough to actually pray and ask God why. Why did He allow this to happen? What was I supposed to do now? I heard the Holy Spirit tell me this: "I never told you to create the course. You were trying to move my hand instead of trusting me to provide!" Astonished by the response I got in prayer, I had to gather myself to accept the harsh reality. Did I ask God, or did I try to play "God?" I remember praying but did I pray and ask God for revelation, or did I just tell Him what I wanted to happen?

But I, the Lord, search all hearts and examine secret motives. I give all people their due rewards, according to what their actions deserve." [Jeremiah 17:10]

I had created a poverty product. The product was created with a spirit of fear attached to it. I failed miserably when trying to make something happen in my natural strength. I want you to think about your last product launch that "failed." Did you seek God for guidance and strategy, or did you just decide that this was what you were going to do? Don't feel bad. We all have done it in an effort to make some quick money. The product concept was solid, but the timing, heart posture, and motive were all wrong!

Although they can make you "some" money, poverty products can hardly ever position you for prosperity. Something in your system is usually broken. Either your pricing is too low, your idea was unoriginal, or the motive behind the release was all wrong. All of this can be rectified by consulting with God and doing some "Prophetic Journaling," a process in which you pray, ask God a question, and write down what you see, hear, or feel in your spirit. If you are launching a product or service to meet a quick need, perhaps it's time to reevaluate.

HOW TO TELL IF YOU ARE SELLING A POVERTY PRODUCT:

- You launched or created it in fear
- You did not pray about it, or you prayed about what you wanted instead of asking what God desired
- You took the idea from someone else. You saw someone selling something, and you were "inspired," aka "copied," and attempted to make it original

- You are experiencing just enough or not enough revenue each month. You are barely covering your expenses, and your revenue is not growing
- Your health is suffering. You are physically or mentally unable to produce the product or service in excellence because of frequent health issues
- You have multiple customer complaints
- You are attempting to meet an urgent need
- You are undervaluing and pricing your products and services
- You rushed through the production and selling process
- You had to lie, steal, cheat, or mislead someone into purchasing from you

PROSPERITY PRODUCTS

Prosperity products are products and services that position you for growth, wealth, and impact. They are often divinely timed and may even show up when you are least expecting them. Although they can be given to you when you are in a time of need, there will be a grace associated with them that will outweigh any spirit of fear, anxiety, or confusion. Prosperity Products come from heaven and not from you! When they come from heaven, heaven's resources will be associated with them.

And God is able to make all grace abound toward you, that you, always having all sufficiency in all things, may have an abundance for every good work [2 Corinthians 9:8, NKJV]

Prosperity Products are created with God, and the fruit is evident. They are typically not an instant fix for your current problem. They are created with longevity and the future in mind. A prosperity product aims to create generational wealth that can outlast you! Prosperity Products also show up with resources and help. When God is creating it, He always releases the money, time, help, location, and wisdom to go along with it.

In everything that he undertook in the service of God's temple and in obedience to the law and the commands, he sought his God and worked wholeheartedly. And so he prospered. [2 Chronicles 31:21, NIV]

In 2021, God placed it upon my heart to lease a commercial space for Beyond The Book Media. I was happily a resident in a small coworking office around the corner from my house, paying a very affordable monthly rent. But yet, I couldn't shake the idea that I needed a much larger space. I began praying and asking for guidance because I couldn't figure out how to afford a bigger space.

I finally took the leap of faith and reached out to a realtor to help me find a location that matched God's vision. I had no idea how it would all work out, but I had faith in God that it would happen. God released to me that I would need a multifunctional space where I could host seminars and worship gatherings and house our corporate office. He also shared that it needed space to record a podcast and shoot content and a large open room to rent out. He was releasing an additional stream of revenue for Beyond The Book Media. I knew this idea had to be divinely timed and created because this was not on my radar.

Most of the commercial spaces were far out of my budget, and I grew frustrated. I went back to God and asked for the monthly rental budget. To my surprise, it was within the rental requirements to lease a commercial space in Alpharetta, GA. I let my realtor know, and we settled upon a unit, a 3000-square-foot suite that met all of God's requirements! I even received a dream the night before telling me exactly how I needed to negotiate the lease terms. And guess what? My landlord agreed to every single one!

It was now time to settle and sign the lease agreement. I had to put my faith in God and not myself. Acquiring this suite would have to be divinely timed because, in my natural strength, I could not afford it nor qualify for it. The day I went to sign the rental agreement, I received a large lump sum of money for an SBA loan that I had applied for months ago. I got enough money to cover the first 9 months of rent. Shortly thereafter, I received another check to cover the renovations needed to make the suite exactly what the Lord had shown me.

God was giving me a Prosperity product with what we named Beyond The Book Media Studios. The resources appeared when we needed them, and the acquisition of the space was divinely timed. There was a supernatural grace that was associated with the entire process. It was not easy, but my faith and execution made it a Godly process. I took Him along the journey each step of the way, and as a result, I was blessed.

You will not have to lack integrity when selling and producing your products and services. Prosperity products will keep you in the will of God, not move you out of it. There are so many "opportunities for entrepreneurship" floating around the internet, but not all opportunities are God opportunities. The promises of quick cash, influence, and power should always be inspected carefully and weighed against Holy Spirit.

HOW TO TELL IF YOU ARE SELLING A PROSPERITY PRODUCT:

- The idea just landed on your lap
- The resources show up when you need them
- They are appropriately priced and valued
- They position you for growth, month over month
- They help others create wealth or transform an area of their life
- It was an original idea that was not "inspired" by someone other than Holy Spirit
- It took faith to create it, and favor showed up through the process
- Although you had to work your faith, there was no toil in its creation
- It was created with the future in mind

IN THE MIDDLE

You can also have a product that is in the middle. It isn't a poverty or prosperity product. I believe many people are here when you are not in lack, but you are failing to see the growth that you know belongs to your business. You have been working on your system or sales process and have gotten results, but you know there is more. It's easy to fall into a space of complacency when you hover in between poverty and prosperity products.

Ask God for an update. Ask Him whether it is time for you to increase your prices or revamp your product offerings. Your season for offering specific products and services may have come to an end. Or it may be time to change up the offerings and the makeup of the product. Perhaps you need a packaging update, a color change, or to add a new product altogether.

Take inventory of all the things you are selling. What's working now and what is not. Don't be afraid to revamp as God leads you. He may be preparing you for a seasonal change in the market. God will allow one area to lack growth to push you into your next big thing. Build in quarterly assessments. Don't grow so comfortable with the old routines that you don't make room for God to do something new in your business.

No matter how we land into entrepreneurship, God wants us to move toward prosperity in every aspect of our lives. Even if you started selling out of desperation and fear, you can transition from poverty to prosperity. Before you launch or sell something, ask yourself if this is a poverty or prosperity product?

Note: Not sure if your product is a prosperity product or poverty product? Check out the quiz on SupernaturaEntrepreneur.co to decide!

You Won't Grow, If You Don't Sow

If you were to survey successful entrepreneurs nationwide, whether they are believers or not, they have at least one thing in common - they are not afraid to invest. Whether they are investing in themselves, their business, or others, the principles of sowing and reaping apply. As a Christian, I have been in church long enough to see this principle practiced when it pertains to giving tithes, offering, and sowing into your local ministry. We discuss giving and investing in church and how we will reap a bountiful harvest. The principle also applies to your business and every area you desire to see an increase.

The Parable of the Sower in Matthew 13 is a great example of sowing and can be applied to entrepreneurship. Let's say you are interested in planting a garden. You begin researching the optimal place to plant your first seeds. You look at many different plots of land and examine the area to determine if your seeds will reap a harvest in that location. You inspect the fruit around each location. At your first location, you notice that the land is dry and barren. Although the area is available for planting, you see no visible signs of any fruit. A decision is made to move to another location because you don't want to waste your time planting in an area that cannot produce.

Moving on to a different plot of land, you see fruit produced, but the fruit is rotten and deformed. You know something was planted, but you can't tell what it is. It appears as if the land is producing sick fruit. Although it is growing, the fruit isn't producing as it was initially intended. Immediately, a decision is made not to plant in this location. You decide to keep on looking. The next plot of land produced beautiful fruit. The fruit looked good enough to pick and eat from afar. Excited, you decided that this is the place, this is the perfect place to plant. Upon a closer examination of the plot of land, you see lots of weeds and bugs camouflaged by the beautiful fruit. Disappointed, because you thought this was the one, the search must continue.

Determined not to give up, you discover a plot of

land with healthy-looking fruit and healthy soil. There are no bugs and weeds, and the fruit looks delicious. This is the perfect spot. Finally, you can plant your garden. You admire the beauty of the flowers and fruit on the land, and you have faith that you have sown into good fertile ground. Grateful that you didn't rush to plant on the first available plot of land, peace and comfort accompany the ability to wait for the harvest. You've sown on good ground, and you can rest in the success of the return on your investment.

As a business owner, it is your responsibility to understand the principles of sowing and reaping and how it applies to your business. Like the planter, you carry a seed, and you will be led to sow your seeds differently. Whether you are sowing (let's call it investing for the sake of this chapter), the initial start of your business, or investing in growing and scaling your brand, your seed and where you sow matter. And there is a sowing strategy you can directly apply to your business.

You are going to have to sow if you want to grow! And again, for the sake of this chapter, we are going to call it investing. You have to invest. If you want to experience supernatural growth, you will have to tap into supernatural principles.

Many first-time entrepreneurs may struggle with

this concept of investing. I know you are wondering, "Where am I going to get the money?" or "Why would I invest money when I am struggling with the money I have right now?" Before you write me off, if you are alive, you are investing in something. Where are you investing, and are you investing in the right places? Are you like the planter that chooses to plant in the barren and dry land? Are you investing in things that are not fruit-bearing? But before we examine where and how you should invest, I need you to understand that investing is biblical. I am going to share a few of my favorite Bible scriptures on sowing and change the word sow to invest so you can make it personal to your business.

Remember this—a farmer who plants only a few seeds will get a small crop. But the one who plants generously will get a generous crop. [2 Corinthians 9:6 NLT]

Remember that a business owner who invests only a few seeds will get a small crop. But the one who plants generously will get a generous crop.

When Isaac planted his crops that year, he harvested a hundred times more grain than he planted, for the Lord blessed him. [Genesis 26:12 NLT]

When the entrepreneur invested in his business that year, he harvested a hundred times more than what he planted, for the Lord blessed him.

For God is the one who provides seed for the farmer and then bread to eat. In the same way, he will provide and increase your resources and then produce a great harvest of generosity in you. [2 Corinthians 9:10 NLT]

For God is the one who provides the investment for the business owner and then bread to eat. In the same way, he will provide and increase your resources and then produce a great harvest of generosity in you.

There were three points I'd like to make from the above scripture references. If you only invest in small amounts, you can expect to receive minuscule amounts to come back to you. But if you invest generously, then you can expect a generous payout. Have you been stingy with your seed? Maybe you are not in a position to invest large amounts, but what is your investing ratio? Are you asking God for something you are unwilling to invest in?

Second, God can multiply your sacrificial investment a hundred times in the same year! When you invest generously, God can give you a supernatural return on your investment that exceeds your expectations. Third, if you ask him, God will give you the money to invest. The money to invest will be in addition to the money needed to keep your business afloat. I find comfort in knowing that I won't be required to invest my last meal away and that God can and will give me the resources to invest. It's up to me to be a good steward of the money, time, talent, and resources.

As simple as put, when you need to see an increase in your life, it's time to start investing! I have a personal investing story I'd like to share. In 2019 in prayer, I was led to attend a business conference. The conference was a $250 investment and two days of my time as a stay-at-home mother of three small children. I had just launched Beyond The Book Media a few months earlier and knew I needed help with my new venture.

Before I attended the conference, I heard Holy Spirit tell me that I was going to join the Business Mastermind coaching program that would be offered at the end of the conference. At the time, my business bank account only had $2,800, and I was pretty sure the program would cost much more than that. I was obedient, and my family agreed to help me with the kids while I made my way to the Buckhead Atlanta Traffic Sales and Profit Live Business Conference.

I sat in a room full of six and seven-figure entrepreneurs, and I enjoyed every bit of it. It was the clarity and strategy I was missing. I felt confident with the new strategy and insights I received and was ready to get back to my team to implement it all! But there was one thing that had to be done before I could leave the conference, I had to join the Business Mastermind.

The presentation was given, and Holy Spirit moved me out of my seat and made my feet walk to the back of the conference room to sign up. What I forgot to mention was that the investment was $15,000 a year or $1,500 a month. I didn't have the $15,000, but I did have enough to make the initial payment. My stomach was in knots, and it took all my strength not to throw up from nervousness. I prayed and asked God to help me get through this signup process and prayed that I didn't hear Him wrong.

I had no idea how I would afford a $1,500-a-month commitment for a business that barely had a sustainable business model. What I knew for sure was that God led me to that conference to do one thing: invest in the Traffic Sales and Profit Business Mastermind Program. God knew that I needed to be surrounded by seasoned entrepreneurs who could help me navigate my business' ups and downs and give me the growth strategy I needed.

I named my seed millionaire and put it back into God's hands. I named it because I knew that this was the seed to me making millions in my business, Beyond The Book Media. Because He told me to invest in it, He would have to see to it that I could stay in it. I had 30 days to make my money back, and I had to trust God through the process. Before the second payment could draft, I launched my first book writing challenge and sold my first self-publishing packages. In one week of selling, I made $7,000, which was enough to keep me in the program for the next 3 months.

Every month, when I thought I wouldn't have enough money to stay a part of the program, God supernaturally would provide the funds to invest. In two years, I'd have enough cash to pay for the program in full without the hassle of monthly install-ments. I went from struggling to pay $1,500 a month to paying my entire program fees in one day! In 2020, I made my first 6 figures as a stay-at-home mom of four (yes, we had another baby).

I think my investment activated a wealth-producing anointing supernaturally and put an urgency on my productivity in the natural. Because I had the $1,500 monthly investment, It helped me think outside the box for revenue-generating strategies. It forced me to level up in my business acumen and understanding. Because I was invested in a five-figure service, it removed the fear of asking others to invest in my high-ticket products and services. My investment positioned me to serve those God assigned to me much better than I would have had the knowledge or ability to. Sometimes God is asking you to invest in yourself and the others assigned to you. The $1,500 was the seed, and Beyond The Book Media reaped the full harvest.

When I started sowing and investing, I knew the principle worked, but I didn't understand how it worked until I read the Parable of the growing seed found in Mark 4:26-29. I believe it lends revelation and understanding on how to partner with God through investing.

26 Jesus also said, "The Kingdom of God is like a farmer who scatters seed on the ground. 27 Night and day, while he's asleep or awake, the seed sprouts and grows, but he does not understand how it happens. 28 The earth produces the crops on its own. First a leaf blade pushes through, then the heads of wheat are formed, and finally the grain ripens. 29 And as soon as the grain is ready, the

farmer comes and harvests it with a sickle, for the harvest
time has come." [Mark 4:26-29]

You are a Kingdom Business Owner inside the Kingdom of God. In this context, you are the farmer, and your business exists to produce fruit on earth by serving and investing in others. Your business harvest is dependent upon the seed you put in the ground. God will give you seed to scatter and to put into the ground - this seed might be money, time, and resources. He will instruct you where and how much to invest. You have to decide to release the seed (put forth the investment) and not hold on to your seed out of fear of failure or loss.

The amazing thing about investing is that you do not have to stop your business from producing to watch your investment. You can invest and sow with faith, knowing that eventually, your seed will grow. The anticipation of when a return on your investment will be made causes many entrepreneurs to rush through their process. It can also cause unnecessary fear and anxiety. If you are sowing and investing Godly seed, you can rest assured that a harvest will come. Don't invest and then stress! Invest your money, time, and resources, and keep building and living as God instructed you.

Many times, God will call you to invest in your

business, and you won't understand all the spiritual momentum behind the harvest. When you invest with God, you will probably have an "I don't understand why" about it. God had me invest my $1,500, and I only had $2,800 in my bank account. I didn't understand why, but I did it anyway. When you invest, He will work out all the details. He doesn't need your help; He just needs your obedience and willingness.

Once you have invested, there is a process for producing your harvest. The harvest is the fruit or results you will receive in your business from your investment. You have to be careful to not try to harvest our produce prematurely. Allow your investment to enter it's through its FULL PROCESS. Once sown, you will begin to see a little leaf blade - signifying that what you have sown is indeed in fertile ground. This is given to you as a sign of encouragement to keep going.

Many people want to harvest the leaf blade. DO NOT DO THIS, for there is more. Then the head of wheat is formed. Your seed is forming and taking shape in the earth. You can see visibly what you have produced - yet it's still not ready for harvest. We can make the mistake of taking the FORM of our harvest because we are impatient.

Finally, the seed is ripe, in its true form. What you

have produced is ready for harvest. Here we can make the mistake of wanting to marvel at the beauty of the harvest. We get excited about the produce. From seed to blade to head to fruit, God did all those things without our help. He was working things out on our behalf. Just as it took work to scatter the seed, so will it cost you to harvest! THE HARVEST COSTS! You must work to gather your harvest!

Let me break this down in a simple step-by-step format to make sure you hold tight to this concept:

1. Identify a need in your business
2. Ask for the money to invest on behalf of that need
3. Find a place to invest that has produced the fruit that you desire
4. Invest and put a seed in the ground in faith and not fear
5. Get back to work and trust that God will supernaturally grow your investment
6. Be encouraged by the initial fruit, but understand that there is more to come
7. Allow for full maturation of your seed, don't pick prematurely
8. Collect your harvest by managing what you have produced
9. Repeat and do it all over again

If you are wondering what and where to sow if you are just getting started, start by sowing into someone that regularly speaks into your life. This can be a one-time thing or consistent giving. I am sure they would love a consistent Cash App notification from you. Another way to start sowing is to invest in books and courses that speak to where you desire to be in your business. You may not yet have the money to invest into full coaching programs, but you can often buy books and courses. Of course, you want to consistently tithe and sow into your church's ministry. If you are growing from the word that is taught and the community that it provides, you need to consistently give.

And finally, you may just have to take a leap of faith and sow into your business in a faith-filled way. Many of us have had to sow our way out of one level and into another. If there is a coaching program or additional training needed, ask God for the strategy on how you can invest. He will tell you where to get the money and release the funds for you to make the move of faith in sowing.

If you are ready to grow, it's time to sow!

Note: If you are looking for a coaching program that is rooted in Biblical Principals and practical strategy, I invite you to learn more and apply to be a part of my coaching and mentorship program The Master's Mind. Visit supernaturalentrepreneur.co for more info.

The Truth About Trailblazing

A trailblazer is a person who blazes a trail for others to follow through unsettled country or wilderness; pathfinder. [Dictionary.com]. As an entrepreneur, you are a trailblazer. You have agreed to do something that probably no one in your family or even close to you has ever successfully accomplished. You have made the decision to follow through the unsettled wilderness of small business ownership, and if I am correct, it was much different than you expected.

I remember when I first cofounded my hair and beauty startup, Myavana. I just knew we were on to something amazing! We had plenty of exposure and funding, and the people loved us! I mean really loved it. I just knew that we'd get a multimillion acquisition by year three, and I'd be sitting in a yacht with my closest friends or jet-setting across the globe. But, of course, that didn't happen the way I envisioned it. In fact, it hardly ever happens the way you envision it. Why? Because trailblazing is about the people you are called to lead and not about you!

God desires to create a legacy from your business, and by doing that, He has to develop and process you into the Kingdom Entrepreneur that He called you to be. Launching your business out of pain, strife, frustration, or selfish reasons is easy. But when God put the desire in your heart, He had so much more planned for you.

I am grateful that God didn't allow my jet-setting lifestyle to happen in year three of my business. I wouldn't have the skills and the strategy that I get to teach thousands of people now. I wouldn't understand the spiritual warfare tactics needed to secure my legacy. I wouldn't feel the value of spending time with God and allowing Holy Spirit to guide my business. As a trailblazer, I learned these strategies while trailblazing. And chances are, you are learning them too.

The first lesson I learned was that trailblazing was a lonely road. As much as I love and appreciate people and community, there were some spaces and places I had to do by myself. My mother, friends, family, and close confidants could not go with me.

Why? Because the assignment was a solo assignment, given to me and to me alone.

And I felt the loneliness. Even as a wife, my husband didn't always understand the vision that God was birthing through me. I'd try to explain what was happening or even solicit advice and help, and he just didn't get it. Heartbroken and frustrated, I'd pull away from God and question if I was even doing what I was supposed to be doing. And time after time, God would send a sign that I was on the right path.

When I got really deep into entrepreneurship, there were sacrifices that I had to make that were uncomfortable but necessary. When God calls you, He will require a sacrifice, usually at the expense of something you love dearly. He needs you to make a decision. Will you choose him, or will you choose your comfort zone? Will you trust that God is with you, or do you need validation from those around you? God will force you into a season of isolation before He launches you out. Even Jesus was forced into isolation, tempted, and tested before He began His great ministry.

Then Jesus, full of the Holy Spirit, returned from the Jordan River. He was led by the Spirit in the wilderness, 2 where he was tempted by the devil for forty days. Jesus ate nothing all that time and became very hungry. [Luke 4:1-2 NLT]

The phrase "everyone can't go" is cliche, but it's the hard cold truth. No matter how tight or cool you are with them, there is a chance they are not allowed on the journey with you. Not because they are evil or trying to cause harm but because they are not called to your trailblazing ministry. The sooner you come to grips with this, the less time you will spend grieving out-of-season relationships!

For some of you, not only are you a trailblazer, but you are the example! Your search for mentorship has come up short because no one has achieved what God has called you to do. God is doing a new thing with you, and He can't risk his investment being tainted by the ideas and motives of others. Before God can release you for mentorship and guidance, He has to ensure you are comfortable with the assignment and who He called you to be. And not rely on the labels others will try to give you.

5 "Before I formed you in the womb I knew you,
before you were born I set you apart;
I appointed you as a prophet to the nations." [Jeremiah 1:5, NIV]

I don't know anyone who does not desire success. Even if you fear success, deep down inside, you are just afraid to fail. We all dream of what success would feel, taste, and even look like! We wait and anticipate success like Cinderella waiting on Prince Charming to carry her away. We are driven and motivated by success; your version of success can differ from another.

Everyone discusses the prospect of success but rarely discusses the pain of success. Success can absolutely suck if you are not ready for it. Once again, I am grateful that our father considers what we can handle when giving out assignments. Often what we are asking for initially, we are not prepared to handle. And when God finally gives it to us, we begin complaining about how overwhelmed we feel, often asking God to take it back. Can you think of a time when you were living in what you prayed for, but you didn't think it would come with all that?!

When you take on too much too soon, there are consequences of success. Are you prepared for what you prayed for? I believe that we desire success, but deep in our hearts, we believe we are undeserving of success. When we finally achieve the success we've dreamed about, here comes overwhelm, depression, frustration, imposter syndrome, doubt, and fear knocking at our door. Success was supposed to cure all of those negative feelings, right? Wrong! Success makes you weigh your new self against your old self and can cause mixed emotions and feelings.

I believe that for every area you are praying for success in, you should equally pray for the success management strategy to go along with it. If you are praying for millions, ask God to equip you with the millions success strategy. Sit down and really consider all that you are believing God for. What are the pros and the cons? How will your life change? How will those around you treat you? Are you prepared for those who aren't as excited about your success? Success is beautiful, and God desires for us to have and maintain success.

The thief's purpose is to steal and kill and destroy. My purpose is to give them a rich and satisfying life. [John 10:10 NLT]

Every trailblazer goes through seasons of isolation and acceleration. Even though isolation is hard mentally, acceleration can be even harder to manage. We have to learn how to steward the acceleration. When I first heard Amos 9:13-15 (MSG), I saw my entire church congregation jump for joy and excitement. When I read it for myself, I had a different reaction. I was going through a season of acceleration and felt the pain expressed in the text.

"Yes indeed, it won't be long now." God's Decree.
"Things are going to happen so fast your head will swim,
one thing fast on the heels of the other. You won't be able to
keep up. Everything will be happening at once—and
everywhere you look blessings! Blessings like wine pouring
off the mountains and hills. I'll make everything right
again for my people Israel:
"They'll rebuild their ruined cities.
They'll plant vineyards and drink good wine.
They'll work their gardens and eat fresh vegetables.
And I'll plant them, plant them on their own land.
They'll never again be uprooted from the land I've given
them."
God, your God, says so. [Amos 9:13-15, MSG]

Most people get excited about the blessings part, and for a good reason. But the part that stood out the most to me was the *"Things are going to happen so fast your head will swim, one thing fast on the heels of the other. You won't be able to keep up. Everything will be happening at once"*. This is what acceleration looks like. When I think about my head swimming and everything happening all at once that I can't keep up,

I a reminded of the uncomfortableness that acceleration brings.

If you are not careful, you could easily confuse acceleration with overwhelm or even doing too much. When you are in a season of acceleration, you can't just give up because you can't keep up. You will need to get yourself together and create a strategy so that you can keep up! You prayed, fasted, and cried out to God for it to come. Now that it's here, you can't fold because it got hard!

When you are in the midst of success, acceleration is evident. Just because God has accelerated you doesn't mean you are void of going through the processing it takes to manage the acceleration. God will bless you and build you at the same time. The lessons that prepare you for the success attached to your obedience are still necessary for your trailblazing journey. The character development that prepares you for the new tables and tax brackets doesn't get eliminated just because you are in acceleration. When praying for rapid success or acceleration, be prepared for rapid testing and overcoming.

God doesn't give his assignments to unprepared and unprocessed people. He will process you in the midst of everything you have going on. So, what does this look like? It looks like Everything great is happening in your business, but at the same time, you have crisis after crisis you have to strategize your way out of. It looks like major press and exposure are released to you, while simultaneously, you find out that you have to let go of one of your employees. It looks like, on the outside looking in, everything is perfect, but mentally and spiritually, you are being challenged in every area!

Once you have come to grips with the idea that you are a trailblazer, you now must manage your trailblazer status. The first thing you will need is a solid community. Find a group of like-minded people. You cannot do trailblazing alone, so don't even attempt it. You may think, "I don't know anyone I can connect with." Well, first, I want to invite you to join us over at Kingdom Business Network! We have over 100k people in our community, and we'd be glad to have you. You can visit www.supernaturalentrepreneur.co for info on how you can connect with us. It's ok to pay for access to community. I've done it, and many other successful business owners have done the same.

Next, you need mentorship and coaching. Much like community, you might have to pay for it. This can be challenging if you are just starting out, but I will give you a pro tip. Find an author with books that speak to your journey, like Supernatural Entrepreneur, and get mentored from afar! Read their books, sign up for their free offers, and follow them on social media. Start using the principles that they share.

Most successful people love to share and give wisdom away for free. Once you've made enough money following their teachings, you can now invest in their paid mentorship and coaching programs! If anything I've shared has resonated with you, visit www.supernaturalentrepreneur.co to learn more about my coaching, consulting, and mentorship programs.

You'll need to take moments to rest and reset. As a trailblazer, you have so much that you are navigating spiritually, mentally, and spiritually! Most people will not understand you. In fact, you will struggle to understand yourself. Your alone time will become sacred. During this time, you will reconnect with yourself and God. If you don't rest and reset, you will burn out! You will begin to resent the call on your life. You will resent the very thing God gave you as a blessing. During your rest time, you can journal, talk to God, read a book, eat your favorite meal, or binge-watch your favorite show. Your brain and body will need this time to recharge - even for us extroverts!!

Understanding what trailblazing, success, and acceleration actually mean will help you understand that you are not alone. Everyone is telling you to feel one way, yet you feel the opposite. The beautiful thing about trailblazing is that you get the opportunity to light the path for others so your family, friends, and loved ones can follow. You were called to lead them, and you are doing just that. Blaze the trail. The world is waiting for you to create the path!

Afterword

While reading this book, I pray that you found revelation for the hard stuff that you have or will experience along your entrepreneurial journey. The chapters discussed in this book were divinely inspired and written to help you think, check your posture, and move you to action. I hope you feel a little bit more normal because running a business can make you think you are crazy!

I have written and published two other books that would be helpful and necessary for your library. I recommend you grab the accompanying journal that will help you think through the concepts in this book and release strategies that will position you for Godly growth. I'd also like you to check out my book, *31*

Prayers For Spiritual Wealth. It is a biblically-based prayer strategy for Christian business owners. I share targeted scripture-based prayers for every area of your business. And finally, please consider ordering my prophetic journal, God Bless The Scribe. It's a journal that you can use to hear the voice of God daily for your business. You can find each of these books on my website - chanelemartin.com.

If this book blessed you, please do me two easy favors. First, grab a copy for your friends and fellow business partners. Second, head to Amazon and leave a review to motivate others to purchase it themselves. You can also learn more about becoming a Supernatural Entrepreneur by visiting our website at SupernaturalEntrepreneur.com.

And finally, did you know that I wrote the first draft of this book in 7 whole days!? That's totally something a Supernatural Entrepreneur would do, right! If you are interested in writing your book in 7 days, I invite you to join Beyond The Book Media's Brand Author Academy (BrandAuthorAcademy.com). It is a writing coaching program designed to help you finish your first draft of your manuscript in just 7 days! We'd love for you to write your next book with us!

God bless you, and may you prosper in all you put your hands to!

About The Author

Prophetess Chanel E. Martin is an award-winning technology founder and the founder of Beyond The Book Media. Martin helps brands write manuscripts in 7 days and publish niche books. Chanel has taught thousands how to complete manuscripts in record time using her book writing formula!

Chanel is also the Co-Visionary of Kingdom Business Network, the largest Christian Entrepreneur Club on the Clubhouse App. Kingdom Business Network, also known as KBN, hosts 14 recurring rooms and reaches over 100K members nationwide! Chanel and her brands have been featured in national publications and broadcasts, including The Real, BET, Black Enterprise, Essence, Ebony, Forbes, Yahoo, Business Insider, and more.

Martin's strategies help each small business owners authentically tell their unique brand story that resonates with their target audience, positions them as an expert, and increases their exposure on and offline. A chemical engineer who holds a master's degree, Chanel has cracked the code on how to successfully brand, fund, and launch small businesses.

As wife and mom of four, Chanel lives by the mantra, "Walk in your purpose and let your light shine." You can learn more about Chanel by following her on all social media platforms @chanelemartin and by visiting her website,_www.chanel-martin.com

Praise for Chanel E Martin

*This book spoke the simple truth that NEEDS to be shared.
No more playing small. Chanel E. Martin the chapter Your
Faith Matters, Your Feelings Don't and Prosperity vs
Provision really blessed me. It's right on time, because God
is calling me to GO AFTER MORE in this season. He's a
God of way more than enough. This book was a nice prac-
tical reminder that my father is King, sovereign over all. -*
Cassandra B.

*Chanel E. Martin!! I just finished reading and it was
Rhema word for me! Oh my goodness! I needed every
sentence for the season that I am in! I felt clearly under-
stood! Thank you! -* **Stevii M.**

*This book breaks the status quo of the misinterpretations
and misused mantras infiltrating the faith community.
Your adequate explanation and scripture prove why those
mantras have held us back as believers. Moreover, how
they are actually instruments of Satan to hinder our
purpose and infect our finances. I loved that it confirms
my convictions and finally someone as successful as you is
reiterating it by experience and exposure.*

Although some of the contexts in the book are known,

*your point of view fills in the pieces we missed or was hidden. This book is filled with so many actionable steps for each chapter which is an excellent addition. I loved every chapter, something was added to previous knowledge and new revelation was revealed. (namely, Provision vs Prosperity) You pinned pointed things I struggle with as an entrepreneur and that is doing the right work. It is an excellent concise manual for Kingdompreneurs but these biblical principles will also help Kingdom employees and all trailblazers. - **Reiandra A.***

*Chanel E. Martin you have done it AGAIN! This book has me repenting and in full surrender in pray to God!!! This is EVERYTHING. When we do it afraid, we forfeit the tools to complete the job! My God! - **Lindsey W.***

This is not a one time read. It's a book to refer to for self-analysis, when strategizing, feeling stuck, etc. I read this book in one day in three sittings, but definitely would reference it.

*I love that this is a practical book (with clear examples) that will help one with growing in faith and confidence, along with Biblical scriptures and references. Too many faith based books not quoting The Word of God for one to learn more on their own. This book gives personal reflections, but leads His people to Him. Thank you Chanel E. Martin. - **Destiny M.***

Bibliography

Provision vs. Prosperity

1. https://www.dictionary.com/browse/provision
2. Exodus 16: 4-5 New Living Translation
3. Matthew 6:31 New Living Translation
4. 2 Corinthians 9:8 New Living Translation
5. Philippians 4:19 New Living Translation
6. John 14:13 New Living Translation
7. https://genius.com/Dottie-peoples-hes-an-on-time-god-lyrics
8. Exodus 16:17-18 New Living Translation
9. Deuteronomy 8:18 New Living Translation
10. https://www.dictionary.com/browse/power
11. Galatians 3:29 New Living Translation
12. Romans 4:16 New Living Translation
13. Genesis 17:6-7 New Living Translation
14. https://www.biblestudytools.com/dictionary/power/

Your Faith Matters, Your Feelings Don't

1. Matthew 22:14 New Living Translation
2. https://www.dictionary.com/browse/toiling

3. https://psychcentral.com/lib/why-are-feelings-important#1

4. https://www.psychologytoday.-com/us/blog/emotional-fitness/201310/feelings-aren-t-facts

5. Ephesians 6:13 New Living Translation

6. 1 Peter 5:8 New Living Translation

Poverty Products VS Prosperity Products

1. Proverbs 10:22 New Living Translation

2. 2 Chronicles 31:21 New International Version

3. 2 Corinthians 9:8 New King James Version

4. Jeremiah 17:10 New Living Translation

5. Joshua 1:9 New Living Translation

Don't Do It Scared

1. 2 Timothy 1:7 New Living Translation

2. Deuteronomy 31:7-8 New International Version

3. Deuteronomy 31:7-8 New International Version

4. Psalm 23:4 New King James Version

5. 2 Corinthians 12:8-10 New King James Version

You Won't Grow If You Don't Sow

1. 2 Corinthians 9:6 New Living Translation

2. Genesis 26:12 New Living Translation

3. 2 Corinthians 9:10 New Living Translation

4. Mark 4:26-29 New Living Translation

The Truth About Trailblazing

1. https://www.dictionary.com/browse/trailblazer

2. Luke 4:1-2 New Living Translation

3. Jeremiah 1:5 New International Version

4. John 10:10 New Living Translation

5. Amos 9:13-15 The Message